Copyright © Bible Pathway Adventures 2017

Author: Pip Reid
Illustrator: Thomas Barnett
Creative Director: Curtis Reid

www.biblepathwayadventures.com

Thank you for supporting Bible Pathway Adventures. Our adventure series helps parents teach their children more about the Bible in a fun creative way. Designed for the whole family, Bible Pathway Adventures' mission is to help bring discipleship back into homes around the world. The search for truth is more fun than tradition!

A catalogue record for this book is available from the National Library of New Zealand.

ISBN: 978-0-473-39927-6

Betrayal of The King

"Yeshua said to him, 'Judas, are you betraying the Son of Man with a kiss?'" (Luke 22:48)

The city of Jerusalem buzzed with excitement. The Feast of Unleavened Bread was about to begin. Every spring, people from far and near came to Jerusalem to keep this special Feast and remember how God had helped their ancestors escape from Pharaoh, the king of Egypt.

"Will Yeshua come to Jerusalem this year?" the people asked. They knew the religious leaders from the Temple did not like this teacher from Galilee. Not only did He teach against their man-made rules and traditions, but many believed He was the promised Messiah, the Savior of the people of Israel.

The religious leaders were worried. "This man has become too popular. The people believe what He says. We must get rid of Him before He turns everyone against us!" But they had to be careful. While Yeshua had many enemies, He also had many friends.

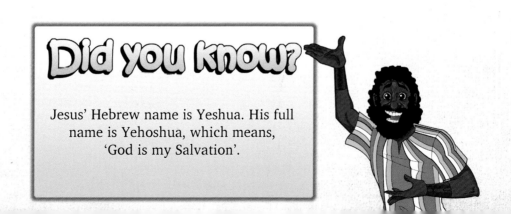

Did you know?

Jesus' Hebrew name is Yeshua. His full name is Yehoshua, which means, 'God is my Salvation'.

As Yeshua and His disciples walked up the road to Jerusalem, He told them what would happen before the upcoming Feast. "The Son of Man will be handed over to the religious leaders. They will sentence Him to death and turn him over to the Romans, who will beat Him, and mistreat Him, and put Him to death. But on the third day He will rise."

Yeshua's disciples were confused. They had traveled around Galilee with Him, listening to His teachings and watching Him perform miracles. "Why does the Master talk about being put to death?" they asked. They did not understand He would die soon. They thought He had come to fight the Roman rulers and become the King of Israel, like King David.

Soon, Yeshua and His disciples arrived in the village of Bethany, near Jerusalem. Yeshua's friend Lazarus rushed out to meet them. Yeshua often stayed with Lazarus and his two sisters, Mary and Martha, when He visited the city.

Lazarus' neighbors stared out of their houses at the famous teacher from Galilee. "Here is the teacher who performs great miracles!" they said. The last time Yeshua visited Bethany, Lazarus had died and Yeshua had brought him back to life. The story of Lazarus had spread far and wide.

That week, Lazarus and his sisters made a special meal for Yeshua and His disciples. After they finished eating, Mary, with tears in her eyes, opened a bottle of expensive perfume. The sweet fragrant smell filled the house as she poured the perfume over Yeshua's feet and dried them with her hair.

"What a waste of perfume," said Judas, one of the disciples. "It could have been sold for lots of money and given to the poor." But Judas did not care about the poor. He was in charge of the disciples' money and wanted it for himself! Looking across the table at Judas, Yeshua said, "She has done this kindness for the day of My burial. You will always have poor people, but you will not always have Me."

Judas sighed in frustration. He had secretly hoped the Master would overthrow the Romans and rule Israel. "Staying around Yeshua is getting 'me' nowhere," he muttered. "He only talks about dying these days. Where is the promised kingdom? Maybe the religious leaders would pay me well to tell them where they can find Him."

That night, Judas hurried through the streets of Jerusalem to the high priest's palace. Inside, the religious leaders were secretly making plans to arrest Yeshua. "The people are beginning to think this teacher is more important than we are. Some even say that He is the Messiah. We must end His life as soon as possible."

"Not during the Feast," said a priest. "Crowds follow Him everywhere. The people may riot if they discover our plan." One of the chief priests nodded slowly. "Let's kill His friend Lazarus, too. They believe what Yeshua says because He raised Lazarus from the dead."

All of a sudden, Judas burst into the room. "What will you give me if I help you find Yeshua?" The chief priest's eyebrows shot up. He couldn't believe his luck! He thought for a moment and said, "Thirty pieces of silver." Judas nodded. Then without another word, he slipped out of the room and into the night. "If Yeshua has truly come to overthrow the Romans, nothing I do will matter," he said. From then on he looked for a chance to betray his Master.

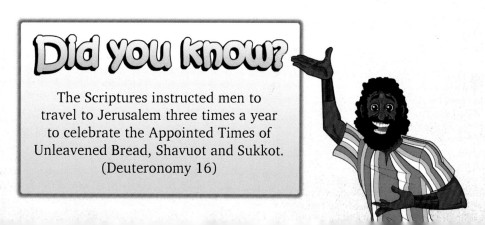

Did you know?

The Scriptures instructed men to travel to Jerusalem three times a year to celebrate the Appointed Times of Unleavened Bread, Shavuot and Sukkot. (Deuteronomy 16)

Early the next morning, Yeshua's disciples found a young donkey for Him to ride on. As they neared Jerusalem, a crowd rushed out to meet Him. "Here is the Messiah," they cried. Waving branches cut down from palm trees, they shouted, "Baruch Haba Be'shem Adonai! Blessed is He who comes in the name of Yah!"

Yeshua's disciples ran ahead, shouting and praising Yah at the top of their voices. "Blessed is the King who comes!" People covered the road with palm branches and clothing to make a royal carpet to welcome Yeshua. "Here is the long-awaited Messiah. Please deliver us!"

A group of religious leaders heard the disciples praising Yah. "Teacher, tell your disciples to be quiet," they said. But Yeshua was not worried. "I tell you the truth. If My disciples were quiet, the very stones would cry out!" More people poured out of the city to see what the fuss was about. "Who is this man?" they asked. "This is the prophet Yeshua, from Galilee. He is the promised Messiah."

Did you know?

A Hebrew day starts and ends at sundown.

Yeshua rode through the city streets to the Temple. Outside, hundreds of Roman soldiers guarded the gates. Pilate, the Roman governor, did not want any bad behavior during the upcoming Feast. Inside, the courtyard had become a marketplace. Traders were buying and selling animals, and changing money. They were cheating the people instead of honoring God. Yeshua clenched His fists. The Temple was never meant to be a place to buy and sell things. It was meant to be place to worship Yah their God.

The next morning, Yeshua returned to the Temple and made a whip out of rope. Cracking it above His head, He kicked over the traders' tables and knocked over their stools. "How dare you turn My Father's house into a market!" He thundered.

Sheep bleated and oxen grunted. Coins scattered across the courtyard and rolled down the smooth stone steps. Yeshua said to the people, "It is written, 'My house is a house of prayer. But you have made it a place for robbers!'" When the chief priests learned what had happened, they were furious. "Let us waste no more time. We must find a way to put this man to death!"

That week, Yeshua visited the Temple to teach everyone about Yah their God. Many people came to hear Him speak and see if He would perform miracles. He told stories to teach the people God's Ways and how Yah wanted them to behave.

When the religious leaders saw the crowds around Yeshua, they sent spies to trick Him with hard questions so they could arrest Him for speaking against God. "Teacher, we know you teach God's laws. Is it against our law to pay taxes to Caesar?" Yeshua knew the religious leaders taught His Father's laws but did not obey them. "Why do you hypocrites try and trick Me? Give to Caesar what is Caesars', and give to Yah what is His."

Another man asked, "Which commandment of God is the most important?" Yeshua answered, "Hear, O Israel. You shall love God with all your heart, soul, and mind. This is the first and greatest commandment. The second is to love your neighbor like yourself. All of God's instructions are based on these two commandments." The religious leaders grit their teeth. Even though Yeshua spoke against their rules and traditions, He still obeyed and taught what was written in the Scriptures. They could not find even one reason to arrest Him.

At the beginning of the day of Passover preparation, Yeshua and His disciples met at a house in Jerusalem for a meal. Yeshua said to them, "I wanted to eat the Passover meal with you before I die. But I will not eat it again until we eat together in my Father's Kingdom." Yeshua took a cup of wine, spoke a blessing, and passed the cup around the room. "Take this and drink it." Then He took some bread and blessed it. "From now on, do this to remember Me." Breaking the bread into pieces, He gave it to the disciples. "Take this and eat it. This represents My body which is being broken for you."

As the disciples ate, Yeshua rose from the table. Pouring water into a basin, He began to wash His disciples' feet. "No," said Peter, one of the disciples. "You shall never wash my feet! This is the work of a servant!" Yeshua answered, "If you do not let me wash your feet, you can no longer be My disciple. I am showing you how to behave."

Then Yeshua said to them, "Tonight, one of you will betray Me." The disciples stopped eating. "Master, who would do such a thing?" They stared at each other suspiciously. "Is it him? Is it me?" Yeshua said, "It is the one to whom I give this bread." He took a piece of bread, dipped it in olive oil and handed it to Judas. "Do what you have to do." It was already in Judas' heart to betray Yeshua. He slipped out of the room and into the darkness. It was time to betray the king.

Yeshua continued teaching His disciples. Then He led them out through the city gates to an olive garden called Gethsemane where He often went to pray. "Tonight all of you will run away and leave Me," He said. Peter shook his head. "Impossible! Even if everyone runs away, I will never leave you!" Yeshua smiled at Peter sadly. "This day before you hear the Temple Crier, you will deny knowing Me three times."

Yeshua took his closest disciples, Peter, James, and John, deeper into the garden. "Wait here. Keep watch while I pray." He walked a little further and fell to the ground. "Father, all things are possible for You. Please don't make Me do this. But I will do what You want Me to do," He prayed. Yeshua understood He was about to die so Yah's promise to restore His people could be fulfilled. Sweat ran down His face like drops of blood and splashed on the ground. He prayed even harder. "If I must die, then let it be according to Your will."

Yeshua returned to the three disciples and found them fast asleep. "Could you not keep watch for even one hour? Keep watch while I pray." Again, for the second time He went away to pray, and again the disciples fell asleep. The third time this happened, Yeshua said, "Get up! The one who is betraying Me is here!"

Through the olive trees, Judas and a group of priests and Temple guards sent by the high priest came toward Yeshua. The flickering light of their torches lit up the garden. Judas had said to them, "The man I kiss is the one you want." He went up to Yeshua and kissed Him on the cheek. "Shalom to you, my Master."

Yeshua stared at Judas calmly. "Do you betray the Son of Man with a kiss? Then do what you need to do." The priests pointed angrily at Yeshua. "Grab Him! Grab that man!" The disciples stared at Yeshua in disbelief. They did not understand what was happening. They still believed their Master had come to overthrow the Romans and become the king of Israel. "Master, shall we fight?" they cried.

Without waiting for an answer, Peter pulled out his sword and swung wildly at a servant of the high priest, cutting off his ear. "Peter, put your sword away!" said Yeshua. "This is what My Father wants Me to do. He would have sent lots of angels if I needed help." He touched the servant's ear and healed him. Then Yeshua turned to the priests. "You came to arrest Me like a thief? Yet I taught in the Temple every day and you did not arrest Me there. But all of this has happened so that My Father's Word will be fulfilled."

The frightened disciples ran for their lives. They were scared the Temple guards would arrest them, too. Everyone ran away, except for Peter and John. They followed Yeshua into the city, keeping in the shadows so they could not be seen.

The guards took Yeshua to the palace of Annas, an important religious leader. Annas was wicked and powerful, and had many Roman friends. Like other religious leaders, he was meant to represent Yah to the people. But the leaders didn't always behave how God wanted them to behave.

Annas asked Yeshua many cunning questions about His teachings to try to trick Him. However, Yeshua was too smart to be trapped by Annas. "I taught in the synagogues and the Temple. I spoke nothing in secret. If you want to know what I said, ask the people who heard Me." Annas paced up and down. His questions did not fool Yeshua. Unsure what to do next, he said, "Take Him to Caiaphas. Let him deal with this so-called Messiah."

Did you know?

The only Scriptures available at the time of Yeshua were what we call the Old Testament. They were known in Hebrew as the Tanakh.

The soldiers led Yeshua to Caiaphas's living quarters where the religious leaders had gathered. Caiaphas, who was the High Priest, said to them, "This man teaches against our rules and traditions. We must find a reason to have Him killed before the people make Him their king." Another priest said, "Let's give some people money to say He is a troublemaker. He looked around the room and lowered his voice. "Then surely the Romans will put Him to death."

That night Yeshua was brought before the Sanhedrin, the Jewish religious council. Determined to find Him guilty, they questioned many men who had been paid to lie about Yeshua. But the stories the men told did not agree. At last, two men stepped forward. "We heard this man say that He will destroy the Temple and rebuild it in three days."

Caiaphas leapt to his feet and peered at Yeshua. "Is this true?" he asked. Yeshua remained silent. Again, Caiaphas asked, "In the name of the living God, are you the promised Messiah?" Yeshua stared straight at Caiaphas. "You are correct. One day you will see Me sitting at the right side of My Father, coming on the clouds of heaven." This was just the moment Caiaphas had been waiting for. "No man can say he is the Messiah!" he shouted triumphantly. "This is blasphemy. He is saying He is God! He must be put to death!"

While the religious leaders questioned Yeshua, Peter warmed himself near the fire in the courtyard below. It was early in the morning, but everyone was wide-awake. Servants hurried to and fro. Guards stood at attention. Everyone knew that something was up. A servant girl guarding the gate stared at Peter. "Aren't you one of Yeshua's disciples?" she asked. Peter shook his head. "No," he told her. "I don't know who you are talking about."

The servant girl wasn't sure if she believed Peter. Speaking to the men standing near the fire, she pointed at Peter and said, "This man is a disciple of Yeshua from Galilee." So they asked him, "Are you one of His disciples?" Again, Peter shook his head. "No, I am not," he said. A little while later, another servant came up to Peter and said, "I saw you in Gethsemane with Yeshua. You must be one of His disciples." Peter turned to the servant angrily. "Look," he said. "I do not know this man!"

Out of the darkness, the Temple Crier's voice echoed over the city. *"All the priests prepare to sacrifice. All the Israelites come to worship."* Peter looked up and froze. Across the courtyard, the guards were leading Yeshua away. At that moment, Yeshua turned and stared straight at Peter. And Peter remembered what He had been told. "This day before you hear the Temple Crier, you will deny knowing Me three times."

Early that morning while it was still dark, the religious leaders took Yeshua, bound and blindfolded, to Pilate, the Roman governor. Although Caiaphas had found Him guilty, only Pilate could have Him put to death. Pilate had come from Caesarea to keep order during the Feast. He often stayed at King Herod's palace when he visited the city.

Outside the palace, Pilate had set up a place to judge prisoners. Each year during the Feast of Unleavened Bread, the Roman governor freed one prisoner chosen by the people. This is where the religious leaders brought Yeshua. Wanting Him put to death as soon as possible, they gave Pilate three reasons to find Him guilty. "This man tells people to disobey the Romans and to not pay taxes to Caesar. He claims He is the king of the Jews."

Pilate was not sure if he believed the religious leaders. He knew they were jealous of this teacher from Galilee. Taking Yeshua aside, Pilate asked, "Are you the King of the Jews?" Yeshua answered, "So you say. This is why I was born and why I have come into the world - to speak the truth." Pilate rubbed his fingers over his chin. "The religious leaders accuse you of many bad things. What do you say?" But to his astonishment, Yeshua kept quiet and did not answer.

Outside the palace, a small crowd had gathered to choose a prisoner. Pilate asked them, "Do you want me to set free Yeshua, the 'King of the Jews'?" The religious leaders stirred up the people to ask for Barabbas, a famous prisoner. The people shouted, "Do not free Yeshua. Free Barabbas!"

Determined to put Yeshua to death, the religious leaders said, "He teaches the people to disobey the Romans. He started in Galilee and now He has come here." On hearing Yeshua had come from Galilee, Pilate had an idea. Herod Antipas ruled the Galilee and had also come to Jerusalem for the Feast. "Take this man to Herod," said Pilate. "He may know what to do."

Herod Antipas was delighted to see Yeshua. He clapped his hands with excitement. "Perhaps this man will perform a miracle for me," he said. He asked Yeshua many questions, but Yeshua did not say a single word. Herod Antipas was not used to being ignored. Slamming his fists on the table, he shouted, "Bring this so-called king a fine linen robe!" But Herod did not want to honor Yeshua. He wanted to make fun of Him.

Did you know?

Gethsemane in Hebrew means 'olive press'. In Yeshua's time, crushing olives in a stone mill and then pressing them under the weight of a beam-press to force out oil produced olive oil.

After Herod Antipas had finished mocking Yeshua, he sent Him back to Pilate to make a decision. "This man has done nothing wrong," Pilate told the crowd. "Even Herod Antipas agrees with me. I will punish Him and set Him free." The religious leaders did not want Yeshua set free. Once again they encouraged the crowd to ask for Barabbas. "Free Barabbas for us!" the people shouted louder than before. "Crucify Yeshua!"

As Pilate gazed out on the crowd, his wife sent him an urgent message. "Leave that innocent man alone. I suffered a terrible nightmare last night because of Him." Pilate cracked his knuckles and thought for a moment. The crowd was growing bigger and bigger. He had to do something before the people started to riot. "Take Him away and whip Him!" he ordered the soldiers.

The Roman soldiers quickly obeyed and took Yeshua to their quarters. They stripped Him, dressed Him in a purple robe, and put a crown of thorns on His head. "All hail the King of the Jews!" they said as they whipped and mocked Him. Then they sent Him back to Pilate, beaten and weary.

Did you know?

The Romans charged people lots of money known as taxes to pay for roads, government, and security. These charges included a water-tax, a city-tax, a road-tax, and a tax on food such as meat and salt.

Pilate sat on the judgment seat outside the palace. Yeshua stood beside him, still wearing a crown of thorns like a king. The crowd pushed and shoved their way forward, shouting, "Crucify Him! Put Him to death on the stake!" Stirred up by the religious leaders, they began to riot. Pilate had to act fast! "Which man do you want me to set free? Barabbas or the King of the Jews?" "Free Barabbas! Free Barabbas!" the crowd shouted at the top of their voices.

"If you let this man go, you are no friend of Caesars," insisted the religious leaders. "The only king we have is Caesar." Pilate glanced at Yeshua. He did not want to send this man to His death. "He has done nothing wrong. Barabbas is the guilty one," he muttered. He stared at the crowd, trying to decide what to do next.

Finally, Pilate rose to his feet. With a heavy heart, he reached for a bowl of water and slowly washed his hands. "I am innocent of killing this man. You kill Him," he shouted to the crowd. "Let His blood be on us and on our children," the crowd shouted back. Pilate could see there was no use arguing with the people. They had made up their minds that Yeshua had to die. Raising his hand to silence them, he made a decision. "Release the prisoner, Barabbas," he shouted. "Crucify the king of the Jews."

THE END

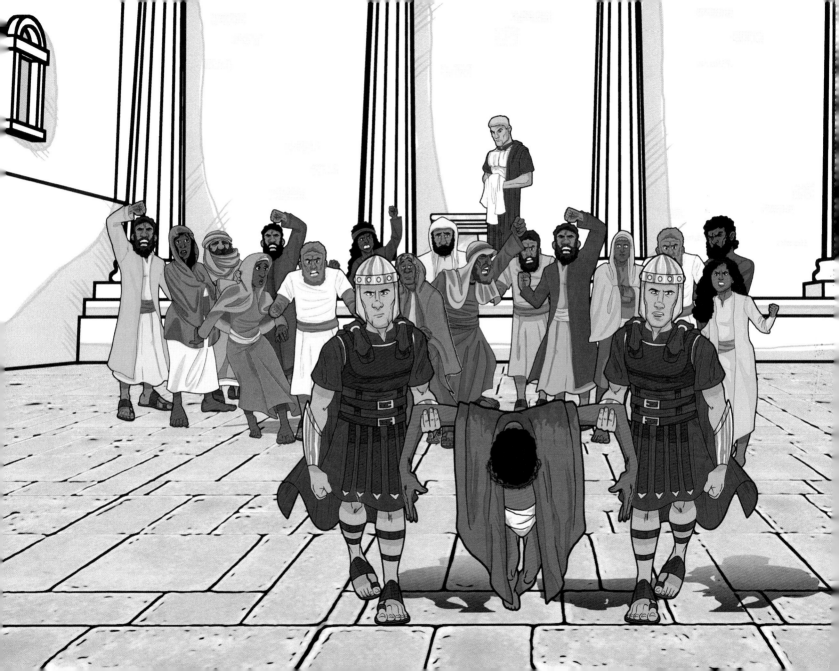

TEST YOUR KNOWLEDGE!

(Match the question with the answer at the bottom of the page)

QUESTIONS

Why did Yeshua travel to Jerusalem? ....

Who poured perfume over Yeshua's feet? ....

At the Temple, what did Yeshua accuse the traders of doing? ....

In which city did Yeshua eat a meal with His disciples before His arrest? ....

What did Yeshua do for His disciples during the meal? ....

In the garden of Gethsemane, how did Judas betray Yeshua? ....

Who appeared to Yeshua at Gethsemane to give Him strength? ....

Which disciple denied knowing Yeshua three times? ....

Which religious leader accused Yeshua of blasphemy? ....

What was the name of the Roman governor who sentenced Yeshua to die? ....

ANSWERS

1. To keep the Feast of Unleavened Bread
2. Mary
3. Turning the Temple into a den of robbers
4. Jerusalem
5. Washed their feet
6. With a kiss
7. An angel
8. Peter
9. Caiaphas, the High Priest
10. Pilate

Discover more exciting Adventures!

Bible Pathway Adventures:

Swallowed By A Fish
The Chosen Bride
Saved by A Donkey
Thrown to The Lions
Witch of Endor
Sold into Slavery
The Great Flood
Shipwrecked!
Path to Freedom
Escape from Egypt
Birth of The King
The Risen King
Facing the Giant

www.biblepathwayadventures.com